How Does the HOLY GHOST Make Me Feel?

Written by *Michele Leigh Carnesecca*

Illustrated by *Carol Shelley Xanthos*

DESERET BOOK

Salt Lake City, Utah

For my children: Brady, Anthony, Brynn, and Cate.
May you always recognize and follow the promptings of the Spirit.
A special thanks to my husband, Chad, for his constant love and support. I love you.
—M.L.C.

To G. and our fabulous five boys for whom I have BIG feelings of love.
—C.S.X.

Text © 2010 Michele Leigh Carnesecca

Illustrations © 2010 Carol Shelley Xanthos

Visit us at DeseretBook.com

Library of Congress Cataloging-in-Publication Data
Carnesecca, Michele Leigh.
   How does the Holy Ghost make me feel? / Michele Leigh Carnesecca ; illustrated by Carol Shelley Xanthos.
      p. cm.
   ISBN 978-1-60641-245-9 (hardbound : alk. paper)
   1. Latter-day Saint children—Religious life—Juvenile literature. 2. Holy Spirit—Juvenile literature. 3. Gift of the Holy Ghost (Latter-day Saint theology)—Juvenile literature. [1. Holy Spirit.] I. Xanthos, Carol Shelley, ill. II. Title.
   BX8643.H63C37 2010
234'.13—dc22   2009038545

Printed in the United States of America   5/2012
Phoenix Color Corporation, Hagerstown, MD

10 9 8 7

Introduction

Heavenly Father wants to give you a very special gift after you are baptized. It is called the gift of the Holy Ghost.

Heavenly Father and Jesus cannot be with you all the time. Because of this, Jesus promised that the Father would send a Comforter, or the Holy Ghost (John 14:26).

The Holy Ghost has many names: the Spirit, the Comforter, the Holy Spirit, the Spirit of God, and the Spirit of the Lord.

The Holy Ghost is "in the form of a man" (1 Nephi 11:11), but He doesn't have a physical body like Heavenly Father and Jesus do. Because He is "a personage of Spirit" (D&C 130:22), His influence can be felt in many places at the same time (see Bruce R. McConkie, *Doctrinal New Testament Commentary* [Salt Lake City: Bookcraft, 1965], 1:738).

If you have not received the gift of the Holy Ghost, you can still feel the power of the Holy Ghost when you hear the truth (Moroni 7:13–17).

After you are baptized, you receive the gift of the Holy Ghost. A worthy Melchizedek Priesthood holder places his hands on your head to confirm you a member of The Church of Jesus Christ of Latter-day Saints and confer upon you the gift of the Holy Ghost (2 Nephi 31:17–18; D&C 20:41).

After you receive the gift of the Holy Ghost, you may have His influence with you all the time, if you truly want it. He will stay with you if you are doing what is right— for example, if you are being kind to others, or listening to good music. The Holy Ghost will leave if you do something that is not right. He will return to be with you again when you repent and begin again to keep the commandments.

The Holy Ghost speaks with a still, small voice. It is like a whisper, but you feel it more than you hear it. When you are quiet and reverent, it is easier to feel and recognize the Holy Ghost. Pray always to have the Holy Ghost with you and to be able to recognize the feelings you receive from Him.

President Gordon B. Hinckley said, "There is no greater blessing that can come into our lives than the gift of the Holy Ghost—the companionship of the Holy Spirit" (*Teachings of Gordon B. Hinckley* [Salt Lake City: Deseret Book, 1997], 259; 3 Nephi 19:9).

Why should I want the Holy Ghost to be with me? And how does the Holy Ghost help me to feel?

The Holy Ghost gives me BIG
feelings of happiness inside.

Doctrine and Covenants 11:13; Acts 13:52

The Holy Ghost helps me feel
warm inside, like when I cuddle up
with my favorite blanket.

Galatians 5:22

The Holy Ghost comforts me when I am sad, just as my family does when I have had a hard day.

Alma 17:10; John 14:27

The Holy Ghost gives me BIG feelings of love for my family, my friends, and EVERYONE.

Moroni 8:26

The Holy Ghost helps me feel like doing good. Serving others is a way I can do good. When I do good things, I feel good inside. When I have these good feelings, I know the Holy Ghost is speaking to me.

Mosiah 5:2

The Holy Ghost gives me feelings of peace during sad times. When my grandma died, I was sad, but I also felt peaceful inside because the Holy Ghost comforted me.

John 14:26–27; Galatians 5:22; 3 Nephi 12:4

The Holy Ghost helps me want to be
a better person, choose the right, and
keep the commandments.

Ether 4:11; 3 Nephi 12:6

When I am lonely, the Holy Ghost helps me feel that I have a friend with me. When I am scared, the Holy Ghost helps me feel calm and safe.

John 14:27

The Holy Ghost helps me know when I have done something wrong. I want to repent and tell Heavenly Father and those I have hurt that I am sorry. I want to make things right with them.

Alma 5:51

The Holy Ghost helps me know that Heavenly Father and Jesus are real and that the gospel of Jesus Christ is true.

3 Nephi 28:11; Doctrine and Covenants 42:17

The Holy Ghost helps me understand the scriptures. I am able to understand things that might be a little difficult to learn.

1 Nephi 10:19; John 14:26

After I have studied a problem out in my mind,
the Holy Ghost will help me know what to do.

2 Nephi 32:5; Doctrine and Covenants 6:15;
Doctrine and Covenants 9:7–9

After I have made a decision, the Holy Ghost gives me feelings of peace, if the decision is right.

If the decision is not right, the Holy Ghost gives me feelings of confusion or uncertainty.

Moroni 10:4–5; Doctrine and Covenants 6:23;
Doctrine and Covenants 9:7–9

I feel good inside when I share my testimony or hear an inspired talk at church. Sometimes I even feel like crying. The Holy Ghost gives me these sweet, tender feelings so that I will know the gospel is true and that Jesus is the Christ.

2 Nephi 33:1; Acts 10:44

The Holy Ghost helps my brother on his mission remember lessons he has learned. The Holy Ghost has helped my brother learn a new language and know what to say to people he teaches.

Doctrine and Covenants 46:24–26; 2 Nephi 33:1

Because the Holy Ghost knows everything,
He helps me know what to pray for.

Doctrine and Covenants 46:30; Luke 12:12

The Holy Ghost can protect me from danger by giving me a warning feeling when I shouldn't go somewhere or do something that would be bad for me.

Sometimes, I even hear a voice telling me what to do.

2 Nephi 5:5–6; 1 Nephi 11:1–11; 1 Nephi 4:6

The Holy Ghost helps me feel patient and forgiving of others. He helps me feel thankful for all that I have.

Mosiah 3:19; Alma 24:8;
Doctrine and Covenants 46:32; Alma 26:16

The Holy Ghost helps me keep the promises I made to Heavenly Father when I was baptized. If I keep my promises to Heavenly Father, He promises me that I will always have His Spirit (the Holy Ghost) with me.

Alma 7:15–16; 2 Nephi 31:17–18; Doctrine and Covenants 20:77, 79

Feelings I receive from the Holy Ghost are called personal revelation. When I receive such feelings, I must listen and obey. When I do, Heavenly Father blesses me.

Alma 5:45–46; Doctrine and Covenants 8:2–3

When I receive impressions from the Holy Ghost, I write in my journal to show Heavenly Father that I am grateful for them. Rereading what I have written about receiving promptings from the Holy Ghost helps my faith grow.

2 Nephi 4:15; 2 Nephi 25:26; 1 Nephi 6:4–6

I am thankful to my Heavenly Father and Jesus Christ for blessing me with the gift of the Holy Ghost.

Moroni 10:5; 2 Nephi 32:5

ABOUT THE AUTHOR

Michele Leigh Carnesecca served a mission in Mexico and received an RN degree from Utah State/Weber State Universities. She currently works for Intermountain Health Care. She has taught classes around the country on women's health issues. She lives in Cedar Hills, Utah, with her husband, Chad, and their four children.

ABOUT THE ILLUSTRATOR

Carol Shelley Xanthos earned her BFA in Illustration from Brigham Young University. She lives with her husband, George, and their five sons in Beaverton, Oregon.